Be Safe!

# Water Safety

by Peggy Pancella

Heinemann Library
Chicago, Illinois

Customer Service  888-454-2279
Visit our website at www.heinemannlibrary.com

Designed by Heinemann Library
Page layout by Roslyn Broder
Printed and bound in China by South China Printing Co. Ltd.

09 08 07 06 05
10 9 8 7 6 5 4 3 2 1

**Library of Congress Cataloging-in-Publication Data**
Pancella, Peggy.
  Water safety / Peggy Pancella.
     v. cm. -- (Be safe!)
  Includes bibliographical references and index.
  Contents: What is safety? -- Learning to swim -- Where to swim -- The buddy system -- Pool safety rules -- Lifeguards -- Protect yourself -- Lake safety -- Rivers and oceans -- Life jackets -- Boating safety -- Trouble in the water -- When to get out -- Safety tips.
  ISBN 1-4034-4936-8 (hardcover) -- ISBN 1-4034-4945-7 (pbk.)
  1. Swimming--Safety measures--Juvenile literature. [1. Swimming--Safety measures. 2. Safety.]  I. Title.
  GV838.53.S24P36 2004
  797.2'1'083--dc22
                                        2003024068

**Acknowledgments**
The author and publisher are grateful to the following for permission to reproduce copyright material:
Cover photograph by Ariel Skelley/Corbis
pp. 4, 20, 21, 24, 28 Corbis; p. 5 Jeff Greenberg/Photo Edit, Inc.; p. 6 James Shaffer/Photo Edit, Inc.; p. 7 Bill Bachmann/Photo Edit, Inc.; pp. 8, 9, 10, 11, 12, 26, 27, 29 Robert Lifson/Heinemann Library; p. 13 Robin Sachs/Photo Edit, Inc.; p. 14 David Young-Wolff/Photo Edit, Inc.; p. 15 Dana White/PhotoEdit, Inc.; pp. 16, 23, 25 Richard Hutchings/Photo Edit, Inc.; pp. 17, 22 Myrleen Ferguson Cate/Photo Edit, Inc.; p. 18 Vito Palmisano/Stone/Getty Images; p. 19 Richard Hamilton Smith/Corbis

Every effort has been made to contact copyright holders of any material reproduced in this book. Any omissions will be rectified in subsequent printings if notice is given to the publisher.

# Contents

Some words are shown in bold, **like this.** You can find out what they mean by looking in the glossary.

# What Is Safety?

It is important for everyone to stay safe. Being safe means keeping out of danger. It means staying away from things or people that could hurt you.

Safety is important in everything you do. One good time to be safe is when you are around water. Water play can be fun if you are careful. Learning some rules about water can help you stay safe.

# Learning to Swim

Many people enjoy playing in water. You will be safer and have more fun if you learn to swim. You can take lessons at a pool or **community center** near your home.

A kickboard or water wings may help you feel safe at first. Soon you will learn to float and to hold your breath under water. You may learn some different swimming strokes.

# Where to Swim

Most pools have **shallow** and deep water. Numbers along the sides tell how deep the water is. Stay in the shallow end until you can swim well.

Always check the water before you swim. Do not get in if you cannot tell how deep it is, or if you are not sure it is safe. An adult can help you decide.

# The Buddy System

A good way to be safe in the water is to swim with a **buddy.** A buddy can be a friend or a parent or other trusted adult.

You should stay near your buddy in the water. You can have fun playing together. If you have trouble, your buddy can help you or call for a **lifeguard.**

# Pool Safety Rules

Most pools have rules for swimmers. You should walk, not run, near the pool. This is so you do not slip and fall. You should keep food and other objects out of the water.

In the pool, do not splash or push others. Try not to bump into other swimmers. Also, stay away from the areas below diving boards, so no one lands on you by **accident.**

# Lifeguards

**Lifeguards** watch swimmers and keep them safe. They help people who have trouble in the water. You should swim only in places that have a lifeguard.

You should obey when a lifeguard asks you to do something. Lifeguards need to **concentrate,** so do not bother them or pretend to be in trouble when you are not.

# Take Care of Yourself

Sunny days are good for swimming, but the sun can burn you even when you are in the water. Always put **sunscreen** on your whole body before you swim. **Waterproof** sunscreen works best.

If you stay outside for a long time, you should put on more sunscreen. You can also use sunglasses, umbrellas, hats, and clothes that cover more of your skin.

# Lake Safety

Swimming in lakes can be fun. The water is usually **shallow** near the shore. See if the water is clean and safe. If you are not sure, do not get in.

Swim near shore where a **lifeguard** can see you. Watch out for sharp or slippery rocks under the water. Do not swim near docks or moving boats.

# Rivers and Oceans

Rivers and oceans look beautiful, but they can be unsafe for swimmers. Strong **currents** in the water can pull you away from shore. Dangerous rocks or animals may be hidden under water.

Never swim alone in rivers or oceans. Stay near shore with an adult who can swim well. Also, try not to swallow dirty or salty water. You could get sick.

# Life Jackets

A **life jacket** is a vest that helps you float in water. If you have trouble, a life jacket can keep you safe until help arrives. Its bright color helps others see you in the water.

Everyone should wear a life jacket for boating, fishing, and other water sports. If you fall into the water, do not panic. Grab onto something, such as your boat or a low tree branch. Then call for help.

# Boating Safety

Riding in a boat is one way to enjoy lakes, rivers, and oceans. Boats can be large or small. You may ride in rowboats, sailboats, motorboats, or **canoes.**

An adult should control the boat. Everyone should wear a **life jacket.** Move slowly and carefully inside small boats, and do not stand up. This can tip a small boat over!

# Trouble in the Water

If someone has trouble in the water, do not get in to help. The person might pull you under water, too. Call a **lifeguard** or other adult for help.

You may reach swimmers near the water's edge with a long branch or pole. You can also throw them a rope or something that floats, like a **life jacket** or kickboard.

# When to Stay Out

Swimming can be fun, but some times are not safe for swimming. Stay out of the water if you see lightning or feel rain. Do not swim at night, either.

Swimming too soon after eating can make you feel sick. Cold water may give you a chill or tire you out. Wait to swim until you feel better and have more **energy.**

# Safety Tips

- Learning to swim is the best way to stay safe in and around water.

- Take a **buddy** when you swim.

- Swim where a **lifeguard** is there to watch.

- Never get in water unless you can tell how deep it is and are sure it is safe. Stay out of water in bad weather, too.

- Always wear a **life jacket** for boating, fishing, and other water sports.

- Use **sunscreen** and clothing to keep yourself safe from the sun's rays.

# Glossary

**accident** something that happens unexpectedly

**buddy** friend or partner

**canoe** narrow boat pushed along with paddles

**community center** place where people in a community gather for activities

**concentrate** pay close attention

**current** flowing movement of water in a certain direction

**energy** power to do something

**lifeguard** good swimmer who watches to keep people safe in water

**life jacket** vest that helps a person float in water

**shallow** not deep

**sunscreen** cream that protects skin from the sun's rays

**waterproof** does not let water through

# Index